Praise for

THE **SHINE** FACTOR

"It's all too easy to get caught up in the day-to-day routine and forget that our job is a vitally important venue for ministry, no matter what our vocation. Kris DenBesten has provided a uniquely creative discussion about putting first things first and focusing on what matters from an eternal perspective."

— Jim Daly, President
Focus on the Family

"Imagine if Christian business leaders would make a commitment to daily live out the fundamentals of their faith. That would be a real game changer. In fact, it could change the world. *The Shine Factor* is an enlightening call to sharpen our focus on what really matters in life. This is the most important book about business you will ever read. I highly recommend it."

— Bill McCartney
Promise Keepers Founder and Chairman Emeritus
NCAA Hall of Fame football coach

"Through a compelling use of scripture and story, *The Shine Factor* cracks open the code on how to serve God and still thrive at work. Scriptural truth and Spirit-led wisdom will challenge you, as it did me, to a deeper view of how to walk with integrity and purpose in the world of work. What a superb expression of God's purpose in work and business!"
— Jerry White, PhD, Major General, USAF, Retired
International President Emeritus, *The Navigators*

"Business leaders face incredible pressure every day. These pressures force a leader to develop character and build capacity or it exposes character flaws leading to failure. In this remarkable business parable Kris DenBesten shows three key questions for character development to guide leaders in building credibility, perseverance and love in order to experience greater success. It's a quick read with timeless applications to deepen the balance in your personal and professional life. I highly recommend it for you and your entire team."
— Dwight Bain, Founder, The Life Works Group

"Through an engaging story, this book addresses what it really means to integrate eternal faith into daily work. This story references Biblical truths and how these enduring truths complement effective management principles. For anyone in the marketplace, striving to make the most of your workday, this book will equip you and encourage you in your faith and work journey."
— Mary Andringa, CEO and Chair of the Board
Vermeer Corporation

"In his latest book, *The Shine Factor*, Kris DenBesten uses a fast-paced parable to illuminate the eternal consequences of our daily business practices. Kris introduces simple yet profound principles that will help the reader make a significant impact in any type of business. This book reveals the fallacies of the "profit at all cost" business philosophy, while replacing it with a practical approach to doing business in a way from which all communities could benefit greatly."

— Rick Boxx, President/Founder
Integrity Resource Center

"*The Shine Factor* is a must read for all aspiring leaders. Its entertaining message challenges readers to view work and life through the lens of eternity and to leave a legacy that shines with the light of Jesus."

— David Wooddell,
The Navigators Workplace Mission, Kansas City

"*The Shine Factor* is a serious page-turner. This book will inspire you to make an eternal difference with your work. It will help you understand the true potential of your life, your work, and your own significance."

— Tim DeTellis, President, New Missions

"What a great story, an easy read with so many practical truths and timeless principles. Anyone who has a heart to know God's purpose for his or her work should read this book. It has inspired and challenged me to make a lasting impact through my business and in my work."

— Don Deluzio, President, Trinity Surfaces

"*The Shine Factor* winsomely and accurately brings to life the very real truth of God's Word applied to life and stewardship for those entrusted with running businesses. From God's eternal perspective, after we trust in Christ, there's no more important step for the Christian business leader than to see their daily interactions with marketplace stakeholders as their primary mission field. Based on their God-given reach, the eternal fruit can be amazing."

— Don Barefoot, President and CEO
C12 Group LLC

"Christian business leaders are positioned to change the culture of the marketplace. Reading the word daily and living it out in the workplace will bring Godly transformation. Exactly how do you go about accomplishing this feat? Read this book! This is a real life road map for transforming the marketplace."

— Raleigh B. Washington, DD, M.Div.
President / CEO
PROMISE KEEPERS

THE
SHINE
FACTOR

FINDING SIGNIFICANCE IN LIFE AND WORK

KRIS DENBESTEN

HIGHERLIFE
PUBLISHING & MARKETING
www.ahigherlife.com

The Shine Factor by Kris DenBesten
Published by
HigherLife Publishing & Marketing, Inc.
100 Alexandria Boulevard, Suite 9
Oviedo, Florida 32765
www.ahigherlife.com

Scripture quotations, unless otherwise noted, are from the English Standard Version of the Bible. Used by permission.

Interior Design: Dimitreus Castro
Cover Design: Emily Conforti

ISBN: 978-0-9907578-6-3
Library of Congress Cataloging in Publication Data

Printed in the United States of America

Table of Contents

Foreword

I FIRST GOT TO KNOW Kris DenBesten several years ago. We met through one of those "coincidences" which only God could arrange. We both quickly realized we had been blessed with a friendship that doesn't take a lot of time to develop, it just is. This happens in the Kingdom, rarely enough to make it precious, but always enriching and ever possible.

As we grew to know each other we found so many commonalities that it was almost eerie. We both had been college-level athletes, both grew up and eventually ran a family business, and both struggled with overcoming performance-based living. We have also both spent years studying and applying Biblical principles to our daily lives. Through these experiences God grew our desire to encourage other business leaders to work for a greater purpose and to experience the joy of glorifying God through business. We are both passionate about sharing this journey of faith for as long as the Lord leaves us here.

Jesus often used parables as He shared His messages of the Kingdom. In *The Shine Factor* Kris has chosen the medium of parable to illustrate the paradigm shift that can transform us from seeking worldly success to seeking eternal Kingdom values. I believe this shift to an eternal focus is one of the most impactful decisions a Christian business leader can make. The lure of material success and the desire for building reputation are key distractions that all business leaders face on a daily basis. I've found that money can never buy what really matters and personal reputation can't fulfill what we truly long for. Ultimately, peace and contentment exist only within a healthy relationship we have with God through Jesus Christ.

If I told you that reading this story and following its principles would make you a mega-millionaire, would you be eager to read it and commit to following though on its concepts? Well, the truth is the payoff that this book highlights is much greater than all the millions this world may have to offer. Those who read it and follow through on it will store up treasures of great value that will last forever. This compelling parable packs the power to change the way you view your life and work!

It is Kris's life journey that has uniquely qualified him to write this book. It's his next step and it's a great one. I am very happy to welcome you to *The Shine Factor*. Enjoy.

Buck Jacobs
Author of *A Light Shines Bright in Babylon, I, Radical, and A Strategic Plan for Ministry*
Founder and Chairman of the Board
The C12 Group, LLC

Introduction

HAVE YOU EVER QUESTIONED whether your time on earth could truly make a difference? How about your work? Does it provide any lasting value? Are you making any significant impact with your life?

My guess is you've pondered these questions more than once.

I've heard that for people who are nearing life's end, the question that haunts them most is, "Did my life really matter?" Nobody wants to reach the end of their earthly journey and realize they've failed to make an impact.

Does the fear of not mattering cross your mind?

Francis Chan, a contemporary thinker and spiritual leader, says, "Our greatest fear should not be of failure but of succeeding at things in life that don't really matter."[1] Fair warning. You are about to read a book by someone who has spent a lot of time succeeding at

1 http://www.goodreads.com/author/quotes/1362751.Francis_Chan

things that don't really matter. I guess that qualifies me as an expert. So please read on.

Early in my career I was a serious S.O.B. (Son of Boss). My dad was a founder of our company, and upon graduating college I found myself taking up space — I mean, working in the family business. One morning while eavesdropping I overheard some fellow employees talking about me: "What a loser." "He will never amount to anything." "He wouldn't even have a job here if his dad didn't own the place." I was clearly making an impact through my work — but obviously not a good one.

Motivation kicked in. I was determined to show those employees that I wasn't a loser. I set my mind on proving I could run this business better than my dad. Years later I closed the biggest deal in the history of our business. I knew my time had come. I was triumphantly singing in my mind, *How do you like me now? How do you like me now?*

When I informed my dad of my great conquest, he shook my hand and congratulated me. The proper response would have been for me to say, "thank you," but I had something else in mind. I held on to his hand, looked him squarely in the eyes, and gloated, "What's the biggest deal you ever closed, Dad?"

His response to my comparison took me by surprise. He thought for a moment and I knew I had him. There has never been a deal bigger than this one. For the moment, I was king. *How do you like me now?*

Then he said it. His words still ring clearly today. With sincerity of heart he replied, "Son, I don't know of a single deal that stands out in my mind. But I guess what I am most proud of is that this company has provided for so many families for so many years. I am just thankful God has allowed me to play a part in it."

How do you like me now?

Thankfully, my dad didn't give up on me. Over the years he has taught me much about life and business. Professionally, I've experienced success beyond what I ever imagined. As a CEO, I've led an amazing team that grew our small company to over $100 million in annual sales. I've also ridden a downturn so steep that we lost over 60% of those revenues in one year — and we lived to tell about it.

Yet — considering the big picture — does any of that really matter?

What truly matters is that my Heavenly Father never gave up on me. He has loved me through both the conquests and the failures. Through prayer, scripture, and life experience, He has taught me much about knowing and doing His will. I've learned that placing my priority on loving Him is the sure way to live a life that makes a difference.

Perhaps the challenges of life and work have caused your priorities to seem out of place. Have you ever desired to spend more time with the ones you love the most? This concept came crashing in on me some years back when my then nine–year-old daughter had a rare virus attack her heart. On Christmas morning in 2008, she was in a coma on full life support. Her doctors told us there was nothing they could do for her. She eventually became part of a medical experiment. An artificial heart — not approved by the FDA at the time — was implanted. This amazing machine kept her alive until she could receive a heart transplant. On April 15, 2009, she received a new heart. She is now a healthy, thriving teenager. (You can check out her story at www.gracyn.org.)

In the midst of her deep crisis, my daughter says she spent some time outside of her physical body. In her words, she died and went to Heaven. There, Gracyn found comfort in an amazing light. The light filled her with faith, hope, and love. It provided the strength and courage she needed for her miraculous recovery. In the story ahead, I describe a powerful light. I didn't make up that part; I used my daughter's own first-hand recollection of what that light is like.

The story you are about to read is a parable that frames some important life lessons along with applicable scripture passages. The fictional characters are based on people from real life experiences. Chances are you will relate to some of the characters and their situations. Stop and reflect as you read. Let the message of this short story resonate in your soul. I pray it will awaken a desire in your heart to make a difference, to leave a legacy, and to live a life that impacts eternity.

It doesn't get much better than that!

THE
STORY

FULLY **1** ALIVE

I T WAS ONE of the most important days in Robert Elder's life. Yet, this morning he didn't have a clue why. Driving with the top down, the crisp morning air invigorated his senses. The finely tuned engine hummed with harnessed power while maneuvering a hairpin curve on Highway 64. The rising sun gleamed between two mountain peaks and was shining directly into Robert's eyes — the light bounced off a mountain stream and illuminated the lush valley floor below. For an instant, the sheer majesty of God's creation dazed him. The awe-inspiring moment uncharacteristically moved him to proclaim, "Thank you, Lord." Robert couldn't recall the last time he'd felt so fully alive.

The scenic Blue Ridge Mountains had offered a much-needed overnight reprieve. His wife and kids would remain in the western Carolinas for a week of hiking, rafting, and other activities. But not Robert — he had too much work to do. *They understand,* thought Robert. *It's my hard work that pays for these nice vacations.* Now it was time to get back to business.

The expensive convertible was just the latest symbol of Robert's blossoming career. His professional climb had been exhilarating; the trophy car was just another fringe benefit of his hard-earned efforts. A smile creased his lips as he dreamed ahead to an Atlanta high-rise. Today's meeting would be the most important opportunity of Robert's illustrious career.

His life was about to change.

Turning east into the light, the penetrating sunrays seemed to be opening a window directly to his soul. It felt good. Reminiscing, the success tasted sweet but it had come at a steep price. This was not the first family vacation he would miss. Cherished moments, ball games, music recitals — all sacrificed — to build the company brand. *Was it really worth it? Was there something more rewarding that he was missing?*

Passing through a small mountain village, a piercing ringtone intruded the solitude. A call from his brother Tom — the perfect remedy — snapped him out of his deep reflection. Though two years younger, Tom had been chosen instead of Robert to lead the family business. Robert had been the company's top rainmaker for years, but apparently that wasn't good enough for Robert's dad. Tom, like his dad, always put people before profits, and focused more on relationships than he did on revenues. Robert contended, *Dad and Tom always cared more about company culture than they did about making money.* Still wounded — but never willing to admit it — he mused, *Dad's biggest mistake. They'd be way more successful had he chosen me to run his company.*

Robert rarely took Tom's calls without making him wait a bit. As he let the call roll over to voicemail, he snickered to himself, *Small time. Tom will never get it as long as he works for Dad's company.*

The boys were inseparable growing up. From the moment Tom took his first steps, the brotherly competition began. Robert was always the better athlete while Tom became the consummate teammate. He always had a knack for making others around him better. Robert smiled big while mentally reliving the district winning shot he hit his senior year. His little brother had thrown him a perfect pass.

They had also complemented each other quite well in the family business. Tom led the support team while Robert's sales abilities brought in the business. Employees called them the dynamic duo. Nevertheless, Robert's ego wouldn't allow him to report to Tom. Not long after the CEO announcement, Robert left the company to set off on his own. Now, in less than six years, Robert's entrepreneurial start-up company was about to dwarf the family business in revenues generated. Plus, today's big deal might produce more profit in one day than the family business could make in a whole month. *There's no stopping me now,* Robert reasoned. *The sky is the limit.*

The hands of time had pushed the brothers apart. Fraternal competition had turned into a fierce rivalry. It had for Robert, anyway. He had become obsessed with outperforming the family business. For him there was much to prove, and after today's conquest everyone would recognize his dominance. Robert kept a keen focus on the financial scoreboard. Now it was time to pile up the points. When it came to making money, the rout was on. Robert wasn't about to throttle back.

THE CALL

Tom's next call was immediate, prompting Robert to pick up the phone. "What's up little bro? Couldn't wait even a few minutes to talk to me, huh?"

"It's Dad," Tom said. "His heart is failing. It doesn't look good. He's fighting to hold on and he wants to see us. Can you get here as soon as possible?"

Before Robert could respond, his phone went quiet. "He what? Where is he? Can he speak?" Nothing but silence.

The awe-inspiring mountain peaks were now a nuisance blocking his cell coverage. Frustration overwhelmed him. *The phone never works up here. Could there be any worse timing?* His mind was racing. With sorrow he remembered how little his father had been around early on. *Living with him was pretty rough. That is, until he found Jesus.*

Robert's dad was tough. He grew up the hard way — scratching and clawing for everything he had. He wasn't much of a father either until Josiah, the company janitor, led him to Christ one morning before work. Robert thought to himself, *Dad never talked much about his childhood yet he probably shared his salvation story a couple zillion times. I wish he'd have come to know Jesus sooner. That sure would have made growing up a lot better.* Robert caught himself. His dad was lying in limbo between life and death yet all he could think about was his own painful childhood memories.

The absentee dad had clearly turned his life around by accepting Jesus Christ as his savior. He took being born again not only in the spiritual sense but also in the literal. It was as if the old man didn't exist anymore and a new man took his place. He transformed into a loving father during his sons' late teenage years. Tom had been way more forgiving of his father's early shortcomings. Although much less merciful, Robert quietly appreciated the changes his dad had made to become a real father.

He glanced down at his phone. Still no coverage. Handling another tight curve with ease Robert sped up while working his way along the serpentine passageway.

OK, I'll high tail it down to Atlanta — catch my meeting — then grab an evening flight to Orlando. Anxiety set in as he reflected on his relationship with his dad. Lately, business had kept them apart. With regret, Robert realized he was now treating his dad much the same way he'd been treated as a child. *Should I skip the big meeting and get to Florida sooner?* It was perplexing. The sports car roared through curves passing numerous cars despite double yellow lines.

Embracing the Christian worldview had reformed his dad on many fronts. It also changed the way he viewed business. Robert's dad believed that his business provided his greatest opportunity to do ministry. "Jesus called fishermen, tax collectors, and business owners as early disciples. He still wants to use us all in the areas where he gives us the greatest influence. For some that is teaching from pulpits, for others it is in foreign missions, for me it is in the marketplace. My business is my ministry."

Robert had heard his dad's speech countless times but had never really bought into it. He attended church — even taught Sunday school for a few years. But he never truly connected to the business-as-ministry thing. Instead, Robert took the easier, more politically correct approach. *You just don't mix business and religion together.* This way of thinking had cost him the top job in the family business. But that didn't really matter much now. Robert's own company was about to become an industry leader.

Tom, on the other hand, had gone "all in." He even considered himself a "steward" of the family business. As a tribute to his father, he was writing a book about *living your faith at work.* It would be based on their dad's life and the biblical principles that guided their company. The writing would be founded on their dad's favorite Bible verse.

What's that verse again? Robert wondered. *Something about letting your light shine before men to glorify your father in heaven.*[2] Glancing down at his phone, it appeared he was receiving a faint signal. He hit the office speed dial button to have his assistant start working on some flight options.

---

2 Matthew 5:16

It was just a quick glance, but at this speed the distraction was multiplied. Adrenaline rushed through his body as he peeked up from the cell phone. The road curved sharply to the right. Robert had crossed the centerline and was racing towards a steep cliff. He stomped on the brake and yanked the wheel hard right. His momentum was too great. Rubber squealed helplessly as tires slid across pavement. The impact was sudden — the sound deafening as an airbag exploded into his face. It enveloped his upper body, shielding him from shattering glass and twisting metal. The racecar bounced violently from boulder to tree as it flipped down the roadside.

Time stood still for Robert Elder.

THE ${3}$ LIGHT

THE EXTRACTION was one of the most challenging the captain could recall in his many years as an EMT. He had seen worse injuries but that was back in his Army days. Since the victim still had a pulse, time was of the essence. It would take the better part of two hours to remove Robert's limp body from the wreckage and hoist him up the hill into the waiting ambulance. The rescue was as exhausting as it was heroic.

From the moment of impacting the guardrail, everything changed for Robert. The brutal crash happened so fast yet it seemed to be moving in slow motion. His ears began buzzing as he was overwhelmed by pain, fear, and deep despair. Vision faded to black as he drifted towards his presumed ending. Alone. Helpless. He was unable to fight back the darkness. In agony, from the depth of his soul, Robert cried out for Jesus to save him.

Suddenly a deep, holy, and pure aura surrounded Robert. It felt like an angelic presence. His fear and pain faded away. He began to experience a new dimension. As though he had travelled back in time, Robert was viewing in his mind's eye the very moment of his salvation. He was a freshman in college home for the weekend. His father had led him to Jesus. With sterling clarity Robert relived that life-changing moment from years ago. He was seeing himself accept Jesus as his Savior. In that very instant he passed from death into eternal life. Right now that was the only thing that truly mattered.

The angelic presence filled Robert's senses with God's word. He could understand it like never before. It was almost as if he was living out the scriptures.

> *The word is near you, in your mouth and in your heart (that is, the word of faith that we proclaim); because, if you confess with your mouth that Jesus is Lord and believe in your*

heart that God raised him from the dead, you will be saved.[3]

A radiant beam washed away the darkness while immersing him in glorious light. The light was blinding, yet he could see like never before. It was as if a veil was lifted so he could see and perceive things in a whole new way. Robert's prior despair turned to euphoria. It was too amazing for words to describe. He didn't just see the light. He could hear it and feel it too. All his senses fused together and erupted with joy. Seeing, hearing, feeling, tasting, smelling — it was all the same. It was perfect.

The angelic presence literally lifted his spirit. It was rising up from his body, leaving the wreckage behind. He ascended through a great tunnel of light at immeasurable velocity. This journey was way beyond exhilarating. Robert felt more than fully alive. He was free!

He continued to see, feel, and hear the light speaking God's word to him. The voice was as beautiful as it was true. The words were alive and packed with power. Unbound by the limitations of flesh and freed from his worldly mindset, all anxiety and every doubt were put to rest by the light that was flooding his soul. *And*

---

3 Romans 10:8-9

the peace of God that transcends all understanding will guard your hearts and minds in Christ Jesus.[4]

The journey through the light tunnel was brief. Or had it been a very long time? Robert wasn't sure. The constriction of time had been left on a mountain top roadway. Regardless, Robert found himself in a pristine heavenly setting. The scenery was beyond belief. A whole new spectrum of color and beauty engulfed him. His greatest moment of worship on earth didn't come close to this. The indescribable light remained constant as songs of praise and thanksgiving radiated continually.

> *To him who sits on the throne and to the Lamb be blessing and honor and glory and might forever and ever!*[5]

Robert could contain himself no longer. He cried out in joy, "I can't believe I am here. How did this happen?"

From the light came a response, *"For by grace you have been saved through faith. And this is not your own doing; it is the gift of God. Not a result of works, so that no one may boast."*[6]

---

4 Philippians 4:7

5 Revelation 5:13

6 Ephesians 2:8-9

Robert realized the voice was an angel that knew him intimately and could communicate directly to his soul. The angel continued, "It is your belief in Jesus as your Lord and Savior that brings you here. Rejoice! Because of His victory over sin and death, the gates of Heaven will be opened to you. It is only by God's grace and mercy that you stand here today. Come with me. I will introduce you to a few others."

As the worship continued, a single voice honed in on him, "Welcome, Robert." He turned and saw someone emerging from a multitude of heavenly hosts. The man looked familiar, but Robert couldn't quite place him.

"It's Josiah, the janitor from your father's business." In that moment it didn't matter that Robert had never really taken the time to know him. The two embraced. "Thank you for sharing Jesus with my dad. It changed his life and then it changed mine!"

Robert was enthused like a little child meeting one of his biggest heroes. "You shared Jesus with my dad, and he shared Jesus with me. If it weren't for you, I wouldn't even be here!" Robert was literally jumping for joy. "I've heard the story a thousand times. Thank you, thank you, thank you!"

"Well, you're welcome," said Josiah. "But I'd say you need to hear the rest of the story. I did share Jesus with your father and he shared Jesus with you. But I take no credit beyond that. You are here because of Jesus Christ. It's what He did that made all the difference. So all those *thank yous* you keep tossing around are bouncing right off me and going straight to Him."

The angelic communication continued. Scripture flowed through Robert's conscience. He grasped each and every word as truth and light. *In Christ Jesus, then, I have reason to be proud of my work for God. For I will not venture to speak of anything except what Christ has accomplished through me.*[7]

Josiah put his arm around Robert. "You're gonna love this. See all these folks gathered around us? They're as excited to meet your dad as you are to meet me. You see, they're all here now because of something God did through your father. Your dad impacted each of them for eternity! Can you believe it?"

"We're all headed to celebrate your dad's arrival. I tell ya, I can't wait to see his face when he realizes what God has done through him. It's way beyond any of his hopes or dreams. Come on along with us. He will

---

7 Romans 15:17-18a

be here in no time. Uh, no pun intended," laughed Josiah. He could tell Robert didn't get it. "There is no time here, Robert. Only eternity. You'll catch on soon enough."

GOOD SAMARITAN

ROBERT COULDN'T CONTAIN his gladness as he and Josiah were swept away with a mighty throng of worshippers. "I had no idea Dad even knew this many people! It's amazing!" Josiah agreed, "Yeah, you've never seen your dad like this before. Things look a whole lot different in the light of eternity!"

Robert soaked in the light as God-directed praise flowed from his heart. He knew he was home. It was Heaven.

"I know he rarely mentioned it to you, but your dad endured many tough times," Josiah lamented. "He was abandoned early and forced to fend for himself.

He pretty much grew up on the streets. It's where he learned to scratch and claw for survival. Maybe that's why he first connected with me. I think he could feel my pain."

Josiah was raised under the strict hand of a hell-fire and brimstone preacher. By early adulthood the only thing Josiah knew about religion was rules. At least, he had become pretty good at breaking them. He rebelled against his dad's religion, chasing the desires of his flesh. It led down a long path of destruction. Eventually he found himself usually homeless, rarely sober, and mostly alone. His family disowned him. Church members would cross to the other side when they saw him. Josiah's life was a mess. That's when God allowed their paths to cross.

"I was sleeping off a rough one out front of your dad's building. He probably shoulda been angry and run me off. Instead he humbly reached down to help me out. At the time I didn't know why. He decided to show compassion for me. He helped me up from my mess and took me to get help at an old warehouse down by the railroad tracks. Your dad was also very generous. He gave a nice donation and asked them to care for me. He was like my Good Samaritan."[8]

---

8 See Luke 10:30-35

Josiah was overcome with gratitude. "I have to tell ya, God does some pretty amazing things at that warehouse.[9] It's where He turned my life around for sure! They cleaned me up and fed me — but it didn't stop there. They didn't just give me a hand-out. They gave me a hand-up!"

Josiah paused, smiled, and continued. "I really needed a job so they sent me to training called Life and Work.[10] That's where I found out how to become more employable. I also learned about God's principles for work." Josiah excitedly shared what he had learned. "I never realized that God, Himself, is a worker. He created us in His own image to work and care for His creation. Did you know work is actually a gift from God?"

Robert shrugged his shoulders and replied. "I guess I've never thought of it that way before."

"Neither had I," admitted Josiah. "My instructor called work a God-ordained opportunity to serve. I'll tell ya something else I learned," Josiah said with passion. "One night after class my instructor asked me if I knew what my name means. Up to that point I'd only brought shame to my name. He told me that Josiah actually means, 'God supports and heals.' Can

9 www.communityfoodoutreach.org
10 www.jobspartnershipfl.org

you believe that? My instructor helped me realize that Jesus Christ was all I needed. That's when everything changed for me."

> *Therefore, if anyone is in Christ, he is a new creation. The old has passed away; behold, the new has come.*[11]

"It took a while, but I made it back to your father's office to thank him. At first he didn't even recognize me. But before I left, he gave me a job." Josiah's toothy grin widened. "That's how I became a God-ordained janitor. Jesus cleaned up my mess so I reckon that qualified me to clean up after others." Robert laughed along with him and said, "Sounds to me like you've done way more than just clean up after others all these years."

Josiah emphatically agreed. "You better believe it! My work was way more than just a job. It was my calling — my opportunity to serve God by serving others. My life became a testimony to how God supports and heals his children. That's how I came to share Jesus with your dad."

Josiah paused to ponder for a moment. "Ya know, it blows my mind that God used your dad to save me.

---

11 2 Corinthians 5:17

Then, He saved your dad by using me. I guess the Lord really does work in mysterious ways."

Robert's comprehension again allowed him to re-live one of his prior life experiences. Robert was taken back to a corporate retreat when he served as a young salesman in the family business. The sales force was seated in a U-shape with his dad in the center. He was passionately sharing his service philosophy with his team. Robert recalled his skepticism at the time. Now it all made perfect sense.

"Many businesses serve only for what it will get them in return. This leads owners and managers to serve strictly for selfish motives. When this happens, a company serves others just so they can sell more stuff. They serve for profit instead of profiting from serving. This can cause employees to view service as just anoth-er duty or an obligation. When we serve only because we get paid to serve, it takes the joy and meaning out of serving others."

Robert's dad paused for effect. He scanned the room, making eye contact with each employee.

"I propose that we as an organization should seek to serve from the heart. Instead of serving for what it will get us in return, let's commit to serve generous-ly by making someone else's situation better. A true servant's heart glorifies God by helping others. The ultimate goal of our service should be to point others towards God's amazing grace: *Each one should use whatever gift he has received to serve others, faithfully administering God's grace in its various forms.*" [12]

Robert's attention returned to Josiah as he continued. "As you can clearly see, your father didn't serve others just to sell more stuff. He served because God called him to serve. He took on a mission to serve God by serving others. That's why he served with such integrity."

Josiah closed his eyes as if he too was reliving a cherished moment in time. "Yes sir, one of my favorite memories of your dad was our Monday morning prayer time. We'd gather to pray each week for the company and the needs of each employee. Your dad knew that prayer was a powerful way he could serve his people."

Josiah couldn't wait to pray with him again.

"Did you know he even paid me to serve a day a week at the warehouse ministry?" Josiah happily answered his own question. "Yeah, he sure did! Your dad wasn't anything like some bosses who expect their employees just to serve them. He believed if he served

---

12 1 Peter 4:10

his employees then they too would be inspired to serve others. The truth is he followed the greatest of all examples! *For even the Son of Man came not to be served but to serve others and to give His life a ransom for many."* [13]

Josiah concluded, "Many of us worshipping with you right now have been touched in some way by your father's servant heart. We are never more like Jesus than when we serve another in His name! When we do this, His mission becomes our mission and we are equipped for service that exceeds all expectations. *Only fear the Lord and serve him faithfully with all your heart. For consider what great things he has done for you."* [14]

Robert basked in the light of this new understanding. His father had used his life and his business to serve God. In doing so, God had used him — to shine the light of Christ — to serve others for God's glory.

---

13 Matthew 20:28
14 1 Samuel 12:24

RICH FOOL

5

As ROBERT GLANCED AROUND he noticed hundreds — maybe thousands — gathering together. All of them shared an amazing sense of pure joy. It was unlike anything Robert had ever experienced. He didn't notice any familiar faces, however, he felt a close bond with each of them. They were all brothers and sisters in Christ. In rich harmony, as with one voice, they glorified God. Robert had never praised the Lord like this before.

Suddenly a familiar face appeared in the crowd. Robert inquired, "Mr. Morley, is that you?"

Mr. Morley was the most successful businessman Robert had ever known. The business school at his alma mater bore the name of Morris T. Morley.

"Yes, it is," replied Mr. Morley. "It is so good to see you again, Robert, especially in the light of this joyous occasion." Robert's mouth jumped in front of his brain and he blurted out, "You look so much younger. And more fit. And I... I didn't even know you were a Christian!"

Mr. Morley laughed forgivingly, "Well. I guess we can thank your dad for helping change that perception. His friendship is one of the highlights of my life. I'm so looking forward to welcoming him home."

Morris Theodore Morley was a brilliant man who finished law school at the top of his class. After a few years of practicing law, he took over a fledgling company that he had once represented. Under his leadership the organization grew into a global giant. Along the way he put his name on many successful endeavors. Morley clearly had the Midas touch. He was also a well-known community leader. From political rallies to football games, the Morley brand was always front and center. Mr. Morley basked in the spotlight. Robert remembered the many lavish parties and benefits he attended that honored Mr. Morley. The guest lists were always a who's who. Robert found the parties to be a networking goldmine.

Mr. Morley recalled, "Your dad was probably the most faithful man I have ever known. He claims it took ten tries before he finally secured his first appointment with me. Well, his patient endurance would pay high dividends. I sensed early on a much greater sense of purpose in our relationship than there is in most business encounters. Your dad was a master at building trust. He eventually became more of an advisor and a business partner than he was a vendor."

Mr. Morley smiled, enjoying the memory of Robert's dad.

"His constant gratitude and consistent follow-up led to many more opportunities. He always placed a high value on our relationship. Never taking anything for granted, he'd work as hard for my next order as he did for my first. We did a lot of business together and I recommended him to many. But that all pales in comparison to what he did for me."

Robert found himself mesmerized as Morley continued.

"Your dad had a heart for helping others rise from poverty. In fact, I think the launch for Morley Food

Bank is the only party of mine he ever attended. It was a huge gathering with the mayor and governor and many other dignitaries. At night's end your dad asked me a question I will never forget: 'Is the underlying purpose of this food center to serve the poor or is it to advance the name of Morris Morley?'"

Morley focused intently on Robert. "Can you believe he asked me that question?" Robert winced and shook his head.

Morley smiled and nodded. "I have to admit — at first — I was a bit taken aback. I mean, who was he to question my motives? But your dad gave me the most sincere look as he pulled a business card out of his wallet. He wrote Matthew 6:2 on the back of the card and handed it to me. He asked me to look up that verse and to call him if I wanted to discuss it further."

Morley's voice was becoming increasingly humbled as he continued.

"It took me a couple weeks, but when I finally got around to reading it the words pierced my heart."

"Thus, when you give to the needy, sound no trumpet before you, as the hypocrites do in the synagogues and in the streets, that they may be

praised by others. Truly, I say to you, they have received their reward." [15]

"I called your dad and asked him to come see me. We had an enlightening discussion about our true purpose in life and work. He challenged me to trust God more than my wealth, to obey His word beyond anything else. Then he did it again. He opened up a Bible and asked me to read aloud."

"A rich man had a fertile farm that produced fine crops. He said to himself, 'What should I do? I don't have room for all my crops.' Then he said, 'I know! I'll tear down my barns and build bigger ones. Then I'll have room enough to store all my wheat and other goods. And I'll sit back and say to myself, "My friend, you have enough stored away for years to come. Now take it easy! Eat, drink, and be merry!"' *But God said to him, 'You fool! You will die this very night. Then who will get everything you worked for?' Yes, a person is a fool to store up earthly wealth but not have a rich relationship with God."* [16]

15 Matthew 6:2
16 Luke 12: 16-21 NLT

The scripture resonated deep within Robert as Mr. Morley continued.

"Talk about looking in the mirror and not liking what you see. I was just like the rich fool! The purpose of my work had been to build my own kingdom and glorify myself in it."

Robert could relate to what Mr. Morley was describing.

"That's when your father explained his company's purpose statement to me: 'We will honor God as faithful stewards of His resources and His relationships.' He clarified that being rich in relationship with God starts with faithful stewardship. A steward recognizes everything belongs to God, including our businesses. He owns it all. Not us! We are just the managers of His possessions. Everything we have comes from Him."

> *"Beware lest you say in your heart, 'My power and the might of my hand have gotten me this wealth.' You shall remember the Lord your God, for it is he who gives you power to get wealth."* [17]

Morley's voice exuded faithfulness. "Since God provides us with wisdom, time, resources, and

---

17 Deuteronomy 8:17-18

relationships, it is our job to honor Him by taking good care of what He entrusts to us. Realizing all blessings come from God opens our hearts to share His blessings with others. Not to draw attention to ourselves, but to give Him the glory for it."

What a change in perspective, Robert thought to himself.

Mr. Morley took on a thankful tone and proceeded. "God is also honored when we show Him gratitude. Any time we take the focus off of ourself and place our focus on Him it becomes an act of worship. Work and worship can become one and the same when we honor God with our efforts. In fact, I've found it's pretty hard to be proud and self-centered while we are worshipping God with gratitude and praise."

> *And whatever you do, in word or deed, do everything in the name of the Lord Jesus, giving thanks to God the father through Him.*[18]

Robert was astonished that his dad had made such an impact on his biggest business hero. *I never knew,* is all he could think as Mr. Morley continued.

"You see, up to that point in my life, everything I did at work was to honor myself. In essence I was

---

18 Colossians 3:17

worshipping me instead of worshipping God. I was experiencing the good but I was missing God's best. That is until your dad enlightened me to seek a new purpose to honor God, glorify Him, and advance His kingdom with my work. *To the King of the ages, immortal, invisible, the only God, be honor and glory forever and ever.*[19]

"I can still clearly hear your father say, 'When we honor God and glorify Him, everything else will fall into place.' Standing with you now — in the light of His glory — I must say, he couldn't have been more correct!"

---

19 1 Timothy 1:17

ETERNAL TREASURES 6

I T WAS A RARE OCCASION for Robert to find himself speechless. "It's amazing what God does when we honor Him with our work," Mr. Morley continued. "As my work became less about me and more about Him, I began to grasp the importance of investing eternally. Many of these souls surrounding us now are benefactors of the eternal investment your father helped spark in me. God has taken that dividend and multiplied it many times over."

Mr. Morley motioned to the crowd for someone to come over. "Do you remember Tex Harris?"

Robert recognized the name. Tex Harris was a football star turned investment broker — a bigger than life self-improvement guru. As a young executive, Robert had attended a workshop led by Tex. It was one of those see-it-then-be-it pep rallies. As Robert thought back to that workshop, he recalled the key points in his mind:

> *It all starts with a vision of excellence. Dream where you want to go and who you want to be. See yourself as a high achieving champion. Prepare an effective strategy and commit to making your dream a reality.*

> *Identify your areas of highest competence. Understand your strengths and weaknesses. Work hard to improve your strengths so you can become great at what you are naturally good at. Manage your weaknesses by teaming with others who are strong where you are weak.*

> *Have the courage to pursue your dream regardless of obstacles. Challenges provide the greatest opportunities to grow and improve. Don't back down when problems arise. Courageously look beyond roadblocks and stay keenly focused on achieving your dream.*

Do what you do best and love doing it. Nothing fuels success like passion. Increasing in knowledge, work ethic, and determination are required for continual improvement, but it is passion that makes the biggest difference. Excellence is found at the point where competence, courage, and passion all intersect.

Robert could visualize and understand things from many years prior. He had just recapped the highlights of an all-day seminar in an instant. It felt surreal.

"Yes, I do remember Tex Harris," Robert proclaimed. "His Improve Continually seminar was excellent. Big Tex was quite an inspiration to me."

"Not nearly as inspirational as your father was to me." Robert turned toward the booming voice. There stood Big Tex Harris with his arms outstretched. He welcomed Robert with a bear hug. "Your dad certainly wasn't big in stature but he was huge in my eyes! Did you know that he and I met monthly with a group of Christian CEOs to help each other grow and improve?"

Robert winced. He recalled how significant that CEO roundtable was to his dad. Robert had assumed it was a waste of time and money.

"Your dad invited me to join his group a few years back. Probably one of the best investments I ever made! It provided something I really needed — accountability! Up to that point not many dared to question Big Tex. But that group was different. We committed to help each other grow personally, professionally, and spiritually. *As iron sharpens iron, so a friend sharpens a friend.*[20]

"We got real. We prayed for each other. We shared advice. Our common goals were to focus on our families, improve our business practices, and grow in our relationship with the Lord. It was probably the greatest team I was ever a part of."

Tex took a moment as if to gather his thoughts. "At one of our meetings your dad led us through an exercise to determine our marketplace ministry potential.[21] We added up the numbers of our employees, customers, suppliers, competitors, and others that our businesses would regularly come in contact with. Those tallies blew us all away. When I added up my potential marketplace ministry opportunity, it was well over fifty thousand people."

---

20 Proverbs 27:17 NLT

21 Buck Jacobs, A Strategic Plan for Ministry (Greensboro, NC, Lanphier Press, 2003), 47

Tex's voice was rising in intensity. "Talk about a mission field! Can you believe my company had the potential to impact that many lives? That's way more than most churches! My business put me in contact with more non-Christians in a month than most church pastors will encounter in a whole year!"

Tex let out a chuckle.

"In my seminars I challenged people to go big or go home. I guess your dad put the money where my mouth was that day. I have to admit, I've invested in all sorts of things over the years — large caps, small caps, ball caps. You name it; I've probably played it." Robert laughed along with Tex.

"But with a ministry potential like that it was high time I started investing in the more important things."

Robert was moved by Big Tex's enthusiasm.

"Your old man was on fire that day! His words are forever etched in my memory."

As Tex continued, both he and Robert visually returned to that moment. Twelve business leaders were huddled around a conference table as Robert's dad read a passage of scripture.

> *"Do not lay up for yourselves treasures on earth,*
> *where moth and rust destroy and where thieves*

> *break in and steal, but lay up for yourselves*
> *treasures in heaven, where neither moth nor*
> *rust destroys and where thieves do not break*
> *in and steal. For where your treasure is, there*
> *your heart will be also.*" [22]

Robert's dad spoke in a matter-of-fact manner. "Let's face it friends, our business is our ministry. For that reason alone, we should strive to do everything with excellence. We need to grow and improve continually — not just for today but also for tomorrow and beyond. *Set your minds on things that are above, not on things that are on earth.*[23] With eternity in mind we can do business for Him. We can give each day our very best for Him. *Whatever you do, work heartily, as for the Lord and not for men, knowing that from the Lord you will receive the inheritance as your reward. You are serving the Lord Christ.*[24]

With passion he implored his peers. "It's time we stop chasing our own temporal dreams and start pursuing God's everlasting vision for our work. His vision reaches beyond the here and now and stretches into eternity. In Christ our eternal future will always be bright. Let's live that way!"

---

22 Matthew 6:19-21
23 Colossians 3:2
24 Colossians 3:23-24

Robert's dad stood and began walking toward the front of the room.

"True excellence is revealed in using our gifts and talents to our maximum potential for God's glory. Nothing could be better than that! We've all got goals and strategies to grow and improve our business. But let's also be willing to set goals and strategies to use our businesses as ministries for God's glory. This will allow us to build great businesses for a greater purpose.[25] We should be proactively investing our time and resources in the things that God cares most about."

As he spoke, Robert's dad wrote four words on a white board and expounded:

> "**Salvation** - Are people coming to know the Lord through our work?
>
> **Sanctification** - Are people becoming more like Christ and growing in relationship with Him through our work?
>
> **Service** - Are people's needs being met in the name of Jesus Christ through our work?
>
> **Sharing** - Are we willingly using our time, talent, and treasure to encourage others in Christ and advance His ministry?"

25 from The C12 Group LLC slogan (www.c12group.com)

Robert thought to himself, *I never really looked at doing business this way. But now I can see how important it is to run a profitable business so that one can continue to invest eternally.* He was proud of his dad's passion for eternity and his influence on others.

Robert smiled as he considered his dad's words. "Treasure sent forward is worth far more than treasure we lay up here. Let's set our hearts on Heaven and be sure we are investing in the eternal things that matter most — the things that advance God's kingdom. God fully expects an everlasting return on the gifts, talents, and resources He gives to us. Improve them continually! Invest eternally!"

> *Then the righteous will shine like the sun in their Father's Kingdom. Anyone with ears to hear should listen and understand!* [26]

---

26 Matthew 13:43 NLT

— BEDROCK GUIDEPOSTS —

BIG TEX NUDGED ROBERT, bringing him back to the present. "Hey dude, remember in my workshop when I asked you to envision what people would say about you at your own funeral?"

Robert laughed. "Yeah, like that matters now."

Tex grinned and continued. "My aim was for people to begin with the end in mind and to work back from there.[27] It was a great exercise to help people set life-long goals. I also encouraged them to clarify core values and develop practical strategies to guide them towards those goals. But knowing what I do now, I didn't challenge them to look far enough ahead. I should've told them to begin with eternity in mind. To look forward

27 Stephen R. Covey, *The 7 Habits of Highly Effective People* (New York, NY: Fireside, 1989), 95

to eternity and what the Lord will reveal about them at their homecoming. That's exactly what your dad is about to experience here. He lived with eternity in mind and soon he will understand just how rewarding that is."

> *So don't make judgments about anyone ahead of time — before the Lord returns. For he will bring our darkest secrets to light and will reveal our private motives. Then God will give to each one whatever praise is due.*[28]

"Now I see that people can be distracted trying to become someone they think they want to be. The values they choose in this pursuit can lead them astray. In the process they may become who they think they want to be — only to miss out on becoming all God created them to be. However, if we take an eternal perspective our values should become bedrock guideposts that direct us towards eternity. Eternal values will guide us to become more like Jesus Christ. That is God's long-range desire for each of us. When God looks at us He wants to see evidence of Jesus in our lives."

Robert nodded. He was surprised at how spiritual Big Tex had become. He listened attentively as Tex continued.

---

28 1 Corinthians 4:5

"When we live by faith, God sends His Holy Spirit to mold and shape us to become more like Jesus. That should be every believer's ultimate goal — to become more like Christ. The Bible clearly explains what that looks like. *But the fruit of the Spirit is love, joy, peace, patience, kindness, goodness, faithfulness, gentleness, self-control; against such things there is no law.*" [29]

Robert responded. "Wow. I've heard that verse many times before but now I finally get it. The Holy Spirit frees us to live as God intends us to live. The more transparent we become, the clearer His values are seen in us. While preparing us for eternity, His Spirit empowers us to become more like Christ. When we navigate by His values, eternal fruit is produced through our lives."

Tex gave him a bone-rattling hug and exclaimed, "Right on, little buddy. Here's something I learned the hard way. Sometimes the best thing we can do is just shut up and let Him shine!" Robert and Tex shared a hearty laugh together. From the crowd a young woman stepped forward.

"Hi Robert, I'm Lily Carson. I want you to know how special your dad is to me. Early in my career I was a sales representative for a well-known insurance

---

29 Galatians 5:22-23

company. I was proposing a health care plan for his company. Everything was going smoothly until he hit me with a surprise question."

Lily's face flushed while she forced a grin.

"He held up my business card and asked me to tell him about our company values. No one had ever asked about that before. Flustered, I fired back the brilliant response, 'That's just something they put on the back of our business cards. I'm not even sure what it says.'

"I finished my presentation and your dad requested I come back in a week. He asked me to research our company values and share with him what I learned. It was a bit surprising, but none of my supervisors knew much about our values either. When I asked why they were printed on our business cards I was told because we've always done that."

Robert shook his head and muttered, "Typical."

"I was very disappointed when your dad chose not to buy from us that day. But, he did take a moment to encourage me. Turns out that moment was pretty impactful!"

Robert and Lily both visualized his dad's modest office. He was sporting his typical work wardrobe, wrinkled khakis and a bland polo shirt. Robert was amused by his dad's lack of concern for outward appearance.

He truly lived by the axiom *it's what's on the inside that counts.* Lily was just one of many vendors with whom his dad had taken time to share his faith.

"Lily, it's a simple issue of integrity for me. I'm concerned about an organization that would put something important like company values on a business card but not teach employees anything about those values. I believe a company with integrity should anchor itself in godly values that have stood the test of time."

Robert's dad wrote three words on a memo pad. He removed the top sheet and handed it to Lily.

> "It all starts out with **clarity**. We need to know what our values are so we can clearly articulate them to others. Next comes **confidence**. We have to trust our values enough to be guided by them and to rely on them in the midst of uncertainty. Finally, we need **conviction**. It's easy to say we have values. We may even print them on business cards or hang them up on the walls of our buildings. But that doesn't mean anything until we commit to live by those values day by day no matter what happens. People believe what they see much more than what they hear."

He looked her in the eyes and spoke with great sincerity. "Lily, you strike me as someone who would desire to build a life and a career on the foundation of godly values."

Robert's attention returned to Lily. She smiled and continued her story.

"Then your dad picked up his Bible and read this to me. *Everyone then who hears these words of mine and does them will be like a wise man who built his house on the rock. And the rain fell, and the floods came, and the winds blew and beat on that house, but it did not fall, because it had been founded on the rock.*[30]

"I never saw him again, but those words stuck with me. A few months later some executives in our company were prosecuted for fraudulent activity. The thing is, if they had just followed the values printed on our business cards, none of that would have happened. In the fallout, many employees lost their jobs. Including me.

"I was a single mom with a young child." Lily paused as her emotions temporarily choked her up. "And, I really needed that job."

She slowly regained her composure and continued.

"As I searched for a new career, a priority became to find a company that was committed to navigate by

---

30 Matthew 7:24-25

values. Eventually I found one and that made all the difference for me."

Lily's face beamed with appreciation.

"One core value of my new company was to care for their employees. A practical way they lived out this value was by retaining a workplace chaplain to support and care for the needs of employees and their families.[31] It turns out your dad also retained this chaplain and recommended the chaplaincy program to my new company."

"That sounds like an excellent employee benefit," noted Robert.

"The best," replied Lily. "In fact, a few years later I suffered a serious medical condition. My work teammates and our chaplain were there for me. Our chaplain gave me a little booklet called Crisis Survival Guide.[32] It was filled with scripture, prayers, and advice on dealing with crisis. It helped me understand how real God is and how He can use our trials to bring us closer to Him. One morning in my hospital room I prayed with our chaplain and accepted Jesus Christ as my Lord and Savior."

Lily choked up with joy. "So did my nine-year-old son!"

---

31 www.chaplain.org
32 Crisis Survival Guide (Facing Crisis Finding Hope) www.gracyn.org

Robert was moved to tears. He and Lily high-fived each other as Lily finished.

"Up until then, I was the type of person who would never even consider stepping foot into a church building. But by the love of a company that was committed to godly values, my son and I found Jesus. Truth is, there's a whole group of us here right now that God reached through that one chaplain. Your dad unknowingly played a key role in that. We just can't wait to thank him and tell him all about it."

Lily cheered, "I am so excited!" as she drifted back amongst her peers.

DEEP FORGIVENESS

LILY'S CONTAGIOUS EXCITEMENT infused Robert. He too couldn't wait to see his dad. He was moved to the limits of emotional ecstasy as he admired the crowd of souls gathering along the shoreline of a glassy sea. He had viewed some scenic coastlines in his day, but none held a candle to this. Robert raised his hands and worshipfully cried out the only words he could muster, "Majesty! Worship His majesty!" It was good.

More and more gathered. The angelic presence alerted Robert it was time to meet another before welcoming his dad.

"Coach Rodgers?" Robert couldn't believe his eyes.

Mal Rodgers was a coaching legend. He had known great success on both the high school and collegiate level. Overall he amassed more than 800 wins, ten state titles, and two national championships. In his second year coaching high school basketball, Coach Rodgers had Robert's dad on his team.

"I had been praying for your dad for many years," explained Coach Rodgers. "I recognized his potential early on but it was hidden beneath his hurt, anger, and insecurities."

Robert grasped the opportunity. "Coach, I know my dad played for you. He talked about it often. But he never really shared anything else regarding his childhood. Any chance you could shed some light?"

"I'd say I'm probably somewhat responsible for that," replied Coach Rodgers. "I taught him that regretting the past bears no lasting fruit. In his case, he needed to release the pain of his past so he could confidently pursue his future. I encouraged him to be motivated by what could be instead of being held back by what was. I'd say he bought into my strategy as much as any player I've ever coached. For years I built my teams on three critical building blocks:

Credibility — hard work, skill, knowledge, strategy, effort

Perseverance — build mental toughness, never give up, fight through challenges, show an enduring attitude

Teamwork — aligning our skills and talents around common goals will allow us to accomplish more together than we would alone."

Coach Rodgers continued with pride. "Despite his lack of size and athleticism your dad became a pretty good ball player. Even more rewarding was how he applied these building blocks in his life to move on from his unfortunate past.

"There was however, one critical element missing in your dad's life at the time. Since he didn't experience much love while growing up, he had a difficult time both accepting and showing love to others. His dysfunctional upbringing left a big chip on his shoulder. This chip was a motivator for sure, but it also kept his account extremely low in relational capital. What that boy really needed was to find Jesus!"

Coach folded his hands and closed his eyes simulating years of prayer. Then he flashed a grateful smile.

"You don't know how thankful I was to learn he finally did. I ran into him a few years ago at the Final Four Basketball Tournament. He was there as a board member of an organization that ministers to college coaches.[33] As we reminisced, he explained how my building blocks had been of great value to his business. We both laughed when he told me he had to tweak those blocks a bit to become more relational."

Robert anticipated what Coach Rodgers was about to tell him. He'd heard his dad explain the relational building blocks many times before. He always considered them kind of corny. But he didn't want to offend Coach Rodgers, so he continued listening intently.

"Your dad called them relational building blocks.

1. Credibility

2. Perseverance

3. Love

He explained there are three relational questions that need to be answered in the course of doing business. Customers, employees, vendors, and fellow teammates are all looking for positive responses to these three questions. Come to think of it, so are our family and friends.

---

33 wwwnationsofcoaches.com

1. Can I trust you?   Credibility
2. Can I count on you?   Perseverance
3. Do you care about me? Love

"When our actions reveal the character traits of the three relational building blocks, the answers to the relational questions are affirmed. This is the foundation for building loyal relationships that could last forever."

Robert understood how important loyal relationships are to growing a business. Yet he'd never considered the potential eternal importance these relationships could carry.

Coach Rodgers waited for his point to sink in. Then he continued, "Did you know your dad started each day praying that the Lord's credibility, perseverance, and love would be seen in him? This empowered him daily to overcome his weakness and excel in relationships.

"I liked the concept so much I started praying for the same things. I then adapted my team building blocks to include love. It's so much easier to build teamwork when everyone cares for each other. Talking about love also gave me a natural way to share my faith with my players. *Let us love one another, for love is from God, and whoever loves has been born of God and knows God... Because God is love.*[34]

"Some of my players are here now because of that decision, and there are many more who will be joining us in the future. Believe me when I say this: If Jesus can change your dad and also change me to excel in relationships, He can do it for anybody."

"I can certainly agree with that," proclaimed Robert. "It sure wasn't easy growing up with..."

Coach Rodgers held up his hand and Robert stopped talking.

"Robert, you've witnessed how your dad became a new man by accepting Jesus Christ as his Lord and Savior. He stopped making excuses and just let Jesus love others through him. It was a clear choice he made. One we all need to make before any of us can truly excel in relationships."

Robert shot back, "That's true, but there are consequences for before..."

Coach Rodgers stopped him again. "You are correct. There are always consequences for our choices. Your dad made some bad ones, especially early on. But in Christ we can all find our forgiveness. Your dad was far from perfect, but he is forgiven by God's

---

34 1 John 4:7, 8b

grace. Don't you think it's about time you forgive him too?"

Robert tepidly replied, "I didn't know I needed to forgive him."

"Robert, you've been carrying a deep-rooted wound for a long time. It's time to let that go, bud. It's a step you must take before you can truly enjoy pure relationships for all of eternity. You need to know, there are no unforgiving hearts in Heaven. There is no guilt, shame, or regrets either. *As the Lord has forgiven you, so you also must forgive.*[35]

"For years you've been trying to prove yourself to others because of how your dad made you feel as a child. Just as he once did, you've made business success the primary driver in your life. This has caused many strained relationships in your lifetime. The root cause of this is that you've never truly forgiven your dad. You've been motivated to outdo him in something that doesn't really matter. That's not good motivation, Robert. I've learned over the years that motivation is simply acting to fulfill an unmet need. *People may be pure in their own eyes, but the Lord examines their motives. Commit your actions to the Lord, and your plans will succeed.*"[36]

---

35 Colossians 3:13
36 Proverbs 16:2-3 NLT

The intensity rose in Coach's voice. "Listen to me, Robert. Only Jesus Christ can fulfill our unmet needs. He has already done that for us. He wants us to release our burdens to Him. In Him there is strength to forgive others because He has forgiven us. His grace is more than enough!"

Robert knew Coach Rodgers was right. He'd been blaming his shortcomings on his dad for far too long. "I will forgive him the moment I see him," Robert promised.

Coach Rodgers smiled. "It's not for him, Robert. He's going to be just fine. Forgiving your dad is for you. All of us here have left our relational hurts and toxic relations in the hands of Christ. Since He has forgiven us, we can forgive those who have caused us relational pain. It's no longer a burden to carry."

"Are you suggesting I need to forgive myself?" Robert asked.

Coach Rodgers put his arm around Robert. "A lot of people know they are forgiven in Christ but they still have a difficult time personally accepting that forgiveness and *letting go* of their pain. They get confused thinking the depth of their sin is too great. But God's forgiveness is deeper than all of our sin, and His love is greater than we can possibly fathom.

"Think about it, Robert. There really is no such thing as forgiving yourself. When Jesus forgives us, we are fully forgiven. It's not something we do for ourselves. It's something He does for us. We just need to personally accept the wholeness of that forgiveness, let go of our past guilt, and take hold of the love and freedom His forgiveness provides. *For freedom Christ has set us free; stand firm therefore, and do not submit again to a yoke of slavery.*[37]

"In Christ we are free. Free of guilt. Free of shame. Free to forgive. Free to love. Free to live for Him. Free to share His relationship with others. You could say the currency of Heaven is measured in relationships. Look around you. God has used your dad in a powerful way simply because he left his past behind, trusted his life to Jesus, and was equipped to excel in relationships."

---

37 Galatians 5:1

FIRST PRIORITY

ROBERT'S NATURAL INCLINATION would have been to defend his prior actions. He would have debated Coach Rodgers about his unforgiving heart. He would have unleashed numerous justifications for why he had behaved as he did. But not anymore.

"I don't have to prove myself to anyone," Robert thought out loud. "There's nothing to justify. I am justified by faith alone. Since God has fully forgiven me I am free from my own sins and free to forgive others." Robert was looking forward to living like this.

Coach Rodgers nodded his approval. "There's one more thing I'd like to share that I know you can relate to. As my coaching success grew, the pressure to win more was amplified. My career took so much time and energy that I had little left for my family and others. My life was way out of balance and I didn't know what to do about it. I shared this dilemma with your dad that day. I will never forget his response.

"He said, 'God never called anyone to live a life of balance. In fact Jesus said, *You shall love the Lord your God with all your heart, all your soul, all your mind, and with all your strength.*[38]

That's not balanced at all. It's radically imbalanced. He wants our all. Everything else can become a distraction if we let it get in the way of our relationship with the Lord. In the long run it really doesn't matter how many games we win, how successful we are, or how much money we make. God only desires that we love Him with all we've got. When we cast our idols aside and simply love Him above all else, He will balance our lives as He sees fit. We aren't capable of balancing our own lives but God can balance our lives for us!'

"Then your dad issued me a challenge. He challenged me to give the first thirty minutes to an hour of each day to growing in my relationship with the Lord. He suggested I read from the Bible, pray, and

---

38 Mark 12:30

journal what God is saying to me through scripture and through prayer.

"When I told him I already wake up at 5:00, he said to make some adjustments in my schedule or I'd have to wake up at 4:00. His point was simple. Beyond anything else, make my relationship with the Lord my first priority every single day.

"Then he made some statement like, 'Priorities are what we do. Everything else is just talk.'"[39]

"Yep. That sounds like my dad," agreed Robert.

"You know what? I gave it a try. It may be the most effective thing I ever did to improve my relationship with God and with others. That discipline to spend the first part of my day with the Lord carried over throughout the day. His presence helped me adjust my schedule and spend more time with those I love. The wins kept coming too. They just weren't nearly as important to me. Loving God became my top priority. He took care of everything else. I realized that for many years I'd been focused on the wrong scoreboard!"

> *But seek first the kingdom of God and his righteousness, and all these things will be added to you.*[40]

---

39 Quote attributed to Buck Jacobs, founder of The C12 Group LLC (www.C12Group.com)

40 Matthew 6:33

Coach Rodgers stepped away. Robert realized he'd also spent a career looking at the wrong scoreboard. Robert's scoreboard had been about making money and putting on the appearance of success. He'd placed way more value on profit than he had on people. He'd clearly elevated revenues over relationships. Ultimately he had prioritized his business success over his relationship with God.

The light was still brilliant and the heavenly setting hadn't changed. It was still as magnificent as ever. Yet Robert was now feeling a sense of unease. He began to ponder in his mind.

It's amazing that all these people have been touched for eternity by my dad. But I haven't met anyone yet who claims to have been touched by me. Why is that? Should I be concerned about it?

The angel knew Robert's thoughts and from the light came answers to his questions. "You and your dad both made the same choice to believe in the Lord Jesus Christ. Because of that choice you are both redeemed by His grace. Rejoice, both of you will be spending eternity with Him in Heaven. Yet, even though you were redeemed in Christ, your hearts were still prone to being self-centered. Part of the mystery of God's ways is that He gives you the free will to choose not only what you believe, but also how you choose to live. Do you seek to follow God's will or do you continually pursue your own self-interests?"

Robert reflected on the question.

Most of his life he'd chosen to focus on himself.

"Your father chose to make his relationship with Jesus the top priority in his life. In doing so, he daily made a decision to let the light of Christ shine in him. God took your dad's obedience and used it to impact many. Consequently, great are his rewards in heaven."

And behold, I am coming quickly, and My reward is with Me, to give to everyone according to his work.[41]

"You chose to let your own light shine most of the time. In so doing you missed out on what could have been. Your own light doesn't draw others to Christ. It only illuminates you and your own self-interests. Your work allowed for much profit. Yet unfortunately you stored up many treasures on earth but you didn't send much treasure ahead."

By now Robert had grown accustomed to communicating with the light. The angelic voice continued to fill him with understanding.

---

41 Revelation 22:12 NKJV

"As with all believers in Jesus Christ, both you and your father will soon stand before the judgment seat of Christ. Here Jesus will reveal to you all the works of your life. The reward will be incredible for each time you allowed God to work through you. Everything else will be judged unworthy and lost for all eternity:

> *But on the judgment day, fire will reveal what kind of work each builder has done. The fire will show if a person's work has any value. If the work survives, that builder will receive a reward. But if the work is burned up, the builder will suffer great loss. The builder will be saved, but like someone barely escaping through a wall of flames.*[42]

"The truth is, distraction is one of the primary tools our enemy uses to derail kingdom-building efforts. First, he tries to deceive people to keep them from believing in Jesus. But once they choose to believe in Jesus and accept His victory, the enemy doesn't go away. He knows he can't steal a believer's salvation. So he changes tactics and uses all means possible to keep them from doing eternal works that God rewards. Robert, God intended your business to be one

---

42 I Corinthians 3:13-15 NLT

of your greatest areas of influence for His kingdom. Unfortunately, you allowed your business to become one of your biggest distractions.

"A sure way to overcome the enemy's distraction is to make your relationship with Jesus Christ the first priority in your life. Devote yourself to prayer and a growing relationship with Him. Then you will desire to do His works that last forever.

> *But whoever does what is true comes to the light, so that it may be clearly seen that his works have been carried out in God."* [43]

---

43 John 3:21

ETERNAL LEGACY 10

ROBERT'S ATTENTION WAS directed towards a majestic throne. There he saw twenty-four elders seated around it. They were dressed in white with golden crowns on their heads. The light radiated from the throne. Robert breathed in deeply as he fell to his knees. He could see, hear, feel, smell, and taste the glory of the Lord. There were no distractions.

> *"The twenty-four elders fall down before Him who is seated on the throne and worship Him who lives forever and ever. They cast their crowns before the throne saying, "Worthy are you Lord and God, to receive glory and honor and power, for you created all things, and by your will they existed and were created." [44]*

44 Revelation 4:10-11

Nothing compares to distraction-free worship! The angel gave Robert a timeless moment to absorb it. Then helped him up and continued.

"Your dad understood that life is full of distractions. Yet, through a growing relationship with Jesus these distractions can be avoided. Some of them can even be transformed into good works that last forever. When we focus on Jesus, He produces good works in us that impact eternity. I've shown you some fruit of these good works so that you too may understand:

- Josiah, the janitor, and Mr. Morley represent **what** Christ followers are called to. When you commit to Christ, His will becomes your will. This allows you to take on His mission to serve others and His purpose to honor God.

- Big Tex and Lily Carson help explain **how** to live out this mission and purpose. Pursuing God's everlasting vision promotes investing eternally. Eternal fruit is produced as you navigate by His values.

- Coach Rodgers represents **why** you are called to live out God's will. When you excel in relationship with Jesus, you are equipped to share that relationship with others. God's love flows through you as He impacts eternity through your relationships with others. By sharing God's love, you can take your faith, your family, and your friends along with you to Heaven."

Robert marveled at how the angel was weaving this all together. As a business leader he fully understood the power of mission, purpose, vision, and values. Tying it all together with loving relationships was brilliant. *I get it now,* thought Robert. *Dad just realized it much sooner than I did.* The truth kept flowing through the light; Robert soaked it all in.

"Your dad's life journey took him through four distinct stages as his career developed. Most people will find themselves pursuing one or more of these objectives throughout their working lives:

Objective 1: Survival
This is working for a paycheck. It is doing what it takes to get by.

Objective 2: Success
This is working for personal achievement. It is doing something for yourself.

Objective 3: Significance
This is working to enhance someone else's life. It is doing something for others.

Objective 4: Shine
This is working to produce eternal fruit. It is letting God work through you for His glory.

"Many people get caught up chasing these first two objectives. This is why work can become so exhausting. Survival is necessary and success can be a good thing provided it doesn't become a distraction. Yet, these two objectives tend to trap a lot of people; they get sidetracked worrying about survival or in chasing success. This leads to self-focus rather than God-focus.

"Those who break through to the third objective open their hearts and minds to focus on others. The fact is a life isn't truly significant unless it positively impacts another.

"The choice to shine is really the big game-changer. Your dad learned that choosing to focus on Jesus Christ would make all the difference. You are standing here today witnessing some of the eternal fruit the Lord will credit to him. By letting the light of Christ shine, your dad was empowered to rise above survival, to soar past success, and to shine beyond significance!"

> *And those who are wise shall shine like the brightness of the sky above; and those who turn many to righteousness, like the stars forever and ever.*[45]

"I wish I'd have known," is all Robert could muster. "I spent my career chasing success. If I knew then what I do now, I would have focused more on others. I would have chosen to shine long ago. I wish my life had borne more eternal fruit."

The angel responded. "It's all right, Robert. Your father's legacy is in great hands. Your brother Tom shares your dad's heart for using business as ministry. He understands that God's Word and the souls of men and women are what last forever. He will continue to run the business accordingly.

"Tom knows the workplace is a vast mission field with countless souls to be reached for Christ. Many more will be joining us over time as your father's business continually shines with truth. Tom has a great desire to share these truths with other business leaders. God will honor that and multiply it.

---

45 Daniel 12:3

"Tom knows business and religion may not always seem to mix well together but he understands that business and our relationship with Christ cannot be separated. A life devoted to Christ cannot be compartmentalized. Jesus Christ is just as much Lord in the Monday morning sales meeting as He is in the Sunday morning church service.

"God can use us most effectively where He gives us the greatest level of influence. Tom will continue to use that influence to do good works that point others to Jesus. *For we are his workmanship, created in Christ Jesus for good works, which God prepared beforehand, that we should walk in them.*[46]

"Rejoice, Robert, God will strategically use the works of your father to impact eternity for many generations to come. His legacy will live on and his rewards in Heaven will grow exponentially."

Robert responded, "I am thrilled for my dad and everything he allowed God to do through Him. But I've done so little. Quite frankly I'm concerned for myself. What will it be like for me when I stand before the judgment seat of Christ?"

"Well Robert — let me be clear — this judgment has nothing to do with your past sins. Jesus has

---

46 Ephesians 2:10

already wiped your sins away and has written your name in the book of life. This judgment is only for believers. It is a judgment based on how you lived your life and how often you glorified God in your works.

"It's clear you now understand your dad's eternal impact. Because of the life he lived, his eternal rewards are vast. But take heart, at the judgment seat of Christ you won't be compared to him or to anyone else. This judgment is all about what you did with what God gave you. It's about your personal stewardship and the motives of your own heart.

"Mere words can't describe how elated you will be to stand before your Lord and Savior. But when all those things you worked so hard for are destroyed by fire you will suffer a sense of great loss. You will be held responsible for every opportunity God gave you while on earth. You will realize what could have been had you chosen to let Him shine rather than chasing personal success. There is no doubt you will wish you'd have done more for eternity.

"But the good news is Jesus won't love you any less than when He sacrificed His own life for yours. You will see and understand everything God has done for you, in you, and through you. Jesus will wipe away your regrets and you will be free to praise Him and serve Him for all of eternity:

> *Behold, the dwelling place of God is with man. He will dwell with them, and they will be his people, and God himself will be with them as their God. He will wipe away every tear from their eyes, and death shall be no more, neither shall there be mourning, nor crying, nor pain anymore, for the former things have passed away."* [47]

---

47 Revelation 21:3-4

SHINE ON

11

GROUP OF TRAUMA SPECIALISTS quickly pored over the file they'd been emailed. The patient had been stabilized and would soon be arriving by medevac helicopter. The prognosis was not good, but this was one of the top trauma units in the entire southeast.

"Oh Lord, My God, I pray that you will work a mighty miracle of healing in the body and mind of this broken child of yours," a trauma nurse quietly prayed as she helped roll the stretcher from the helicopter. The Life Flight EMTs had already revived the patient twice before landing on the rooftop of this high-rise Atlanta hospital. The unconscious accident victim was barely clinging to life.

"This one just doesn't want to die!" proclaimed one of the medevac EMTs.

Immediately, the expert trauma team sprung into action. "Hang in there buddy! Hang on!" the surgeon mumbled while shining his light into a dilated pupil.

The light soothed and comforted him, however, Robert couldn't stop thinking about what could have been. *How could he have believed in Jesus but not been willing to use his greatest source of influence — his business — to glorify God? Why hadn't he produced more eternal fruit, especially in his own family? He could have done so much more.* Robert longed for another chance, but he would never choose to leave these glorious surroundings.

He jubilantly anticipated his father's arrival. *How will Dad react when the host of saints and angels welcome him home? I can only imagine how Dad will respond when he enters the joy of the Lord and hears his Savior say well done!* Robert turned towards the throne and peered across the water.

*From the throne came flashes of lightning,
and rumblings and peals of thunder, and
before the throne were burning seven
torches of fire, which are the seven spirits
of God, and before the throne there was
as it were a sea of glass, like crystal.*[48]

Indescribable. Inexpressible. Unspeakable. He
bowed to his knees! This was far beyond what
he could ever envision. Robert fell prostrate and
savored the pure majesty of the light. His heart
joined the throng in heavenly worship.

*Holy, holy, holy, is the Lord God Almighty.
Who was and is and is yet to come.*[49]

Of all his injuries, it was the head trauma that most
concerned the medical staff. The attending neurosur-
geon explained the post-surgery prognosis to Robert's
wife, Jennifer. "You never know what to expect with
this type of brain injury. We don't know if he will
regain consciousness. If he does, he may not be able
to move the right side of his body. We are also very
concerned that he may not be able to speak again. The
next 48 hours are critical."

---

48 Revelation 4:5-6a
49 Revelation 4:8b

The news was difficult to take. Jennifer's heart sank as she approached her two children asleep in waiting room chairs. She whimpered quietly as her motherly compassion flowed though her. *The vacation cut short. The frantic dash to Atlanta. News of their grandpa's passing. The scary trauma surgery. How could she now possibly explain their dad's situation? It was all so tragic...so sad. What else could go wrong?* She was clearly on the verge of an emotional meltdown.

That's when it happened. It wasn't an audible voice — but her mind was filled with a message. It was scripture she'd heard before — now it spoke directly to her. *Be still and know I am God.*[50] *Wait for the Lord; be strong, and let your heart take courage; wait for the Lord!* [51] The message inspired her. It encouraged her. Jennifer gently put a hand on the shoulder of each child. She began praying for a miracle with all of her heart.

As she prayed, her faith grew stronger.

"Lord, I don't know what to do but I know that you do. I place the outcome of this trial in your hands. You are my refuge and strength. I ask for a miracle that will glorify you, fulfill your will, and point others to you.

---

50 Psalm 46:10
51 Psalm 27:14

I know you have an eternal plan and that your timing is perfect. So Lord, in you I will wait.

I wait in faith…
>Knowing you are in control.

I wait in confidence…
>Knowing you are almighty.

I wait with expectancy…
>Knowing your plan is perfect.

I wait in thankfulness…
>Knowing you are worthy.

I wait in dependence…
>Knowing you are all I need.

And I wait in stillness…
>Knowing you are my God."

If given a choice, Robert would have remained where he was. But it wasn't his time. The buzzing in his ears returned as he felt a falling sensation. As his plunge continued, the light began washing away. His euphoria faded as the light steadily diluted. It was no longer indescribable. It was just normal. The source of this light was a lamp above his head.

What had happened to him? Was his afterlife experience real... or was it just a dream? Had he really been to Heaven or was it just a vision?

As the fog cleared, Robert knew he had returned to his earthly body. His senses were coming back. Eventually he realized he was in a hospital bed. His eight-year-old daughter, Maggie, was touching his hand and crying, "I love you daddy. Please come back." Her sadness gripped his heart. Robert wanted to say I love you and assure Maggie it would be all right. But he just couldn't put the words together. He tried to squeeze his right hand around hers but he couldn't make it move. That's when Robert felt the light again for a brief moment. *Arise, shine, for your light has come, and the glory of the Lord rises upon you.*[52] The presence of the light touched him. He knew it brought healing.

He'd been given another chance.

Robert rejoiced in the gift of life. This time he will make it count. He will prioritize his relationship with the Lord. He will let the light of Christ shine in him for God's glory.

Robert will start today with his family. He'll carry this same light to his business, his church, his commu-

---

52 Isaiah 60:1

nity, and anywhere else God may give him influence. Robert will do more than live life to the fullest. He will live life like he will live forever. He will let God impact eternity through him.

Tears of joy welled in Robert's eyes as he lifted his right hand heavenward. With sterling clarity he proclaimed his new life verse, *Let your light so shine before men that they will see your good works and glorify your Father who is in Heaven.*[53]

It was one of the most important days in Robert Elder's life. And now he clearly knew why.

---

53 Matthew 5:16

Conclusion

ROBERT'S RECOVERY — though long and painful — was deemed a medical miracle. Doctors could not explain how he survived and overcame the injuries he had sustained. The prayers of his friends and family lifted him. Knowing God listened, they prayed together often. The prayers brought them together in unity. In the midst of their crisis they found hope. Through adversity their faith was strengthened.

Robert knew his life was a miracle from God. He had been healed in every way possible. Each morning he took the first hour of his day to spend time alone with God. Through prayer, scripture, and reflection, his relationship with God became his first priority. Robert discovered that the more time he spent with the Lord, the more his closest relationships improved. This allowed Robert's faith, family, and friends to become the centerpieces of his life. Robert was motivated and empowered by the eternal work God was doing through him.

His glorious preview of eternity revolutionized Robert's perspective on life and work. Instead of prioritizing profit, he began to focus on people first. He understood the importance of profit. It is needed to keep an organization alive. But people are the lifeblood of any organization. Profit is like oxygen. As oxygen supports life, profit supports the people. Robert realized the more profit growth he could generate the more people he could help. This perspective changed Robert's heart for business. He quit trying to become an industry legend and focused more intently on serving God by serving others.

Tom knew the change in his brother could have only come from God. They both agreed that faith in Jesus Christ was the foundation of their lives and work. On this foundation the brothers came together. They chose to merge Robert's company with the family business. Tom proved an excellent CEO. Robert focused on sales — which is what he always did best. The company thrived. They both used their unique giftedness to steward the business for God's glory.

Both brothers were humbled by how many lives their company would impact. Robert was thankful that God allowed him to be a part of it.

Together they built an enduring company based on the eternal principles that Robert learned in the light. These principles attracted others. They became a lamp to their feet and a light for their path. Through good times and bad, pursuing these principles kept them on target. The family business faithfully carried out their dad's legacy to shine.

Serve others

Honor God

Invest eternally

Navigate by His values

Excel in relationships

From Heaven their dad rejoiced. Most importantly, their Heavenly Father was pleased as many of His children were impacted for eternity.

Eventually, like-minded successors were trained to carry the torch ahead. The brothers transferred a significant portion of their company stock to a Christian foundation.[54] This assured that ministry would continue in their business long after they were gone.

---

54 National Christian Foundation (nationalchristian.com)

Robert's experience in the light changed the way he viewed his life and work. Most importantly it transformed the way he lived. By God's grace Robert lived a life that mattered. He loved God. He was loved by his family. His eternal rewards are plentiful. Like his dad, Robert was empowered by the light to rise above survival, soar past success, and to shine beyond significance.

Good news! This same light is as available for us today as it was for Robert.

> I am the light of the world. If you follow Me,
> you won't have to walk in darkness, because
> you will have the light that leads to life.[55]

Yes, we too can live a life that matters. Once we accept the eternal salvation found in Jesus Christ, we become one of His light-bearers. Our instruction is not to hide His light but to let it shine. He calls us to be a light to the world and a lamp in our own home. The darkness cannot stop us because God provides the light we need. By His power we reflect His glory. As we carry this light on our own journey, the world around us becomes brighter as He impacts eternity through us. The light of Christ — alive in us — is the shine factor.

---

55 John 8:12 NLT

Reflection

Chapters 1-3

Robert's scoreboard was clearly focused on personal success. He was willing to sacrifice relationships with his brother, father, wife, and kids to appease his ego and run up the score on his financial scoreboard.

- What does your life's scoreboard look like? In other words, what do your actions show is most important to you?

Robert's dad believed that his business was his ministry. Robert initially believed that business and religion should not be mixed.

- What is your perspective on this concept? What are some ways God could use your work for ministry?

Romans 10:9 says, *If you confess with your mouth that Jesus is Lord and believe in your heart that God raised him from the dead, you will be saved.*

- What do you believe about Jesus, salvation, and eternal life?

Chapter 4

A Christ-like heart glorifies God by helping others:

Serve Others
    Humility — Put others first
    Compassion — Show you care
    Generosity — Exceed expectations

Accept His **mission** to serve others:

> *For even the Son of Man came not to be served but to serve others and to give His life a ransom for many. Matthew 28:20*

1. Josiah viewed his work as a mission to serve God by serving others. Can you think of some ways God could use you to serve others in your work?

2. What is the difference between serving for profit and profiting from serving?

Chapter 5

A Christ-like soul obeys God's purpose in life and in work:

Honor God
Stewardship — It's all His
Trust — Obey His word
Gratitude — Worship Him

Fulfill His **purpose** to honor God:

And whatever you do, in word or deed, do everything in the name of the Lord Jesus, giving thanks to God the father through Him. Colossians 3:17

1. Mr. Morley's perspective on his purpose for work changed from honoring himself to honoring God. How did he do this? How could you do this?

2. Do you think God has a purpose for your life and work? What could that purpose be?

Chapter 6

A Christ-like mindset prepares us for eternity:

Invest eternally

Excellence — Your best for His glory

Growth — Improve continually

Passion — Where your heart is your treasure follows

Pursue His **vision** to invest eternally

Whatever you do, work heartily, as for the Lord and not for men, knowing that from the Lord you will receive the inheritance as your reward. You are serving the Lord Christ. Colossians 3:23-24

1. Is there anyone in your life who is committed to helping you grow personally, professionally, and spiritually? What are some actions you can take to grow and improve the gifts God has given you?

2. God expects an everlasting return on the gifts, talents, and resources He gives us. What are some things you can do to send treasure ahead by investing eternally?

Chapter 7

Christ-like values direct our path:

Navigate by His values:

    Clarity — Know your values

    Confidence — Trust your values

    Conviction — Live your values

Embrace His **values** to produce eternal fruit

> *But the fruit of the Spirit is love, joy, peace, patience, kindness, goodness, faithfulness, gentleness, self-control; against such things there is no law. Galatians 5:22-23*

1. Tex tells Robert that he wished he would have encouraged people to begin with eternity in mind. What does that mean to you? How would a focus on eternity impact the way you live today?

2. What are your core values in life and work? Are those values guiding you to produce eternal fruit?

Chapter 8

Christ-like relationships last forever:

Excel in relationships:
Credibility — Do I trust you?
Perseverance — Can I count on you?
Love — Do you care about me?

Relationships are the currency of Heaven

*Let us love one another, for love is from God,
and whoever loves has been born of God and
knows God…Because God is love. 1 John 4:7-8*

1. Is there any relational baggage from your
   past that is holding you back? Perhaps
   someone you need to forgive? If so, how
   can you move beyond this?

2. How would those closest to you answer
   these relational questions?
   • Do I trust you?
   • Can I count on you?
   • Do you care about me?

Chapter 9

"A sure way to overcome the enemy's distraction is to make your relationship with Jesus Christ the first priority in your life. Devote yourself to prayer and a growing relationship with Him. Then you will desire to do His works that last forever." Pg. 81

You shall love the Lord your God with all your heart, all your soul, all your mind, and with all your strength. Mark 12:30

1. How could loving God with everything you have lead to a more balanced life?

2. What are the biggest distractions in your life that are keeping you from growing in relationship with God? How can you overcome these distractions?

Chapter 10

"God will strategically use the works of your father to impact eternity for many generations to come. His legacy will live on and his rewards in heaven will grow exponentially." Pg. 88

> *For we are his workmanship, created in Christ Jesus for good works, which God prepared beforehand, that we should walk in them. Ephesians 2:10*

1. Have you ever thought of yourself as God's work of art? (His workmanship created to do His work.) How does that make you feel about your work?

2. Share an example of something you do now that leads to a long term benefit or reward later. How does this principle apply to the concept of sending treasure ahead to eternity?

Chapter 11

"Robert rejoiced in the gift of life. This time he will make it count. He will prioritize his relationship with the Lord. He will let the light of Christ shine in him for God's glory." Pg. 96

Let your light so shine before men that they will see your good works and glorify your Father who is in Heaven. Matthew 5:16

1. Where has God given you influence in your life? What can you do to let His light shine where He has placed you?

2. Will you commit each day to seek God and allow Him to impact eternity through you? How will you do this?

Many of you upon finishing *The Shine Factor* may be thinking, *Wouldn't it be great if I could work at a Christian company?* Or maybe you are already contemplating this excuse, *If only I worked for a Christian company, then I could really let my light shine.*

Stop right there!

In reality, there is no such thing as a Christian company. There are companies owned by Christians. Some may even profess that God owns their business. There are companies that strive to operate by Christian principles. Some companies develop a God-honoring Christian culture within their organization. But there are no Christian companies — just Christians and non-Christians who work there. This is where you come in! God wants to use you within your company and your community to impact others for eternity.

Perhaps your work environment seems very dark. **Don't wait around hoping to work for a Christian company. Be the light for those around you. Let His light shine right where you are.**

It is my goal that in reading *The Shine Factor* you will be encouraged to let the light of Christ shine in you regardless of your current circumstance.

If you'd like help in taking the next step towards putting The Shine Factor to work, go to www. shinevision.com.

- For business owners — It will encourage and help you to design a corporate culture that allows for the light of Christ to be seen in your organization.

- For Christian business leaders — It will direct you to lead others by following biblical principles.

- For Christians at work — It will help you seek Christ and encourage others to do the same at life and work.

There are numerous organizations committed to helping you live your faith at work. Many of them were referenced in *The Shine Factor*. For a list of those organizations and recommended resources that can help you on your faith and work journey please go to http://www.shinevision.com.

Acknowledgements

Thank you to the many who helped much in the development of this story. These are a few who stand out.

My Lord and Savior Jesus Christ – You are my all in all. I pray my life story brings you glory!

My wife Robin – You inspire me more than you know. I love you.

My kids, Cole, Gracyn, and Brooks – You make me proud. Being your dad is one of my life's greatest joys.

Merle DenBesten – thanks for your patience and your Christ-like example. I am blessed to have parents like you and my mother Fran DenBesten to look up to.

Buck Jacobs – There is much of you in this story. You've been a great mentor and I am thankful that God has put us on this journey together.

Dr. Jim Henry and Dr. David Uth – Your spiritual leadership has made a lasting impact on my life. I am thankful for the many years that both of you have been my pastor.

Marilyn Jeffcoat ~ You are simply the best. If it weren't for you I'd still be wondering if maybe I should write a book some day.

Dave Welday, Liza Mena, Chris Maxwell and the entire Higher Life team ~ Thanks for pulling this all together and keeping it on schedule despite my constant "tweaking."

Scott Coley ~ One of the joys of leadership is handing off tasks to someone who does them much better than I do. Thanks for your willingness to "lead up."

Mel Bokhoven ~ I doubt I'd even work at Vermeer Southeast had it not been for you. Thank you for believing in me when most people didn't!

Mary Andringa ~ You have been an inspiring mentor to me for many years.

Vermeer Southeast employees ~ You are the best. I am blessed to be on the same team with you. Shine on!

CONTINUE THE CONVERSATION

If you believe in the message of this book and would like to share in the ministry of getting this important message out, please consider taking part by:

- Writing about *The Shine Factor* on your blog, Twitter, Instagram and Facebook page.

- Suggesting *The Shine Factor* to friends and send them to the author's website www.shinevision.com.

- When you're in a bookstore, ask them if they carry the book. The book is available through all major distributors, so any bookstore that does not have it in stock can easily order it.

- Encourage your book club to read The Shine Factor.

- Write a positive review on www.amazon.com.

- Gather a group of friends and/or coworkers to read and discuss the book together.

- Purchase additional copies to give away as gifts.